jazz blues

Arranged by Brent Edstrom and James Sodke

T0055414

ISBN 978-0-634-05880-6

7777 W. BLUEMOUND RD. P.O. BOX 13819 MILWAUKEE, WI 53213

Visit Hal Leonard Online at
www.halleonard.com

contents

ALL BLUES

By MILES DAVIS

AU PRIVAVE

By CHARLIE PARKER

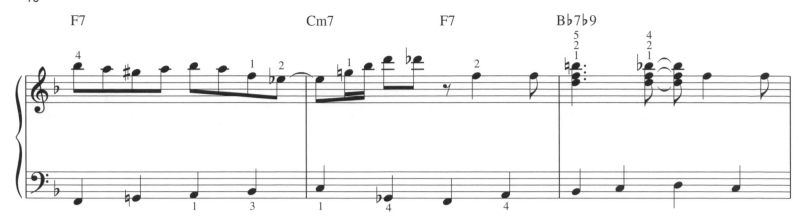

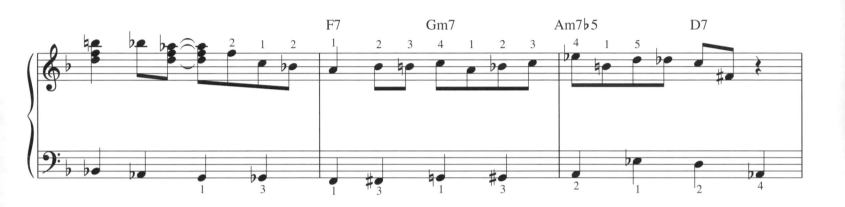

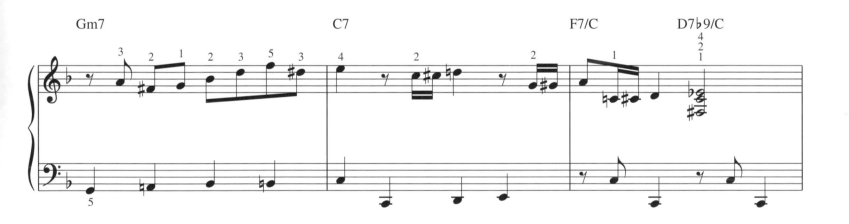

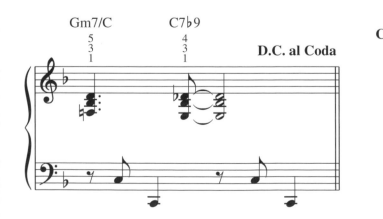

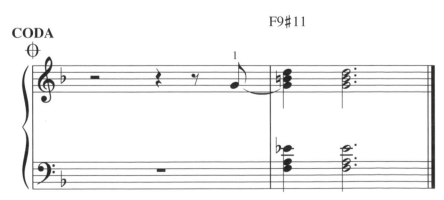

BILLIE'S BOUNCE
(Bill's Bounce)

By CHARLIE PARKER

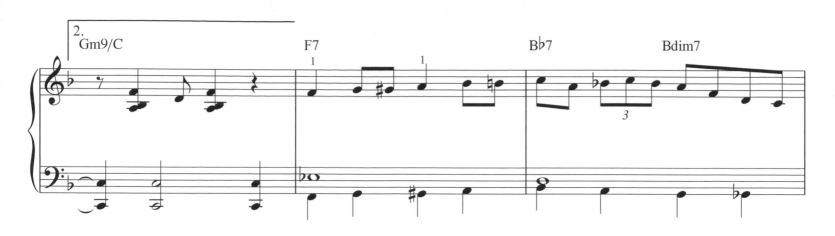

BAGS' GROOVE

By MILT JACKSON

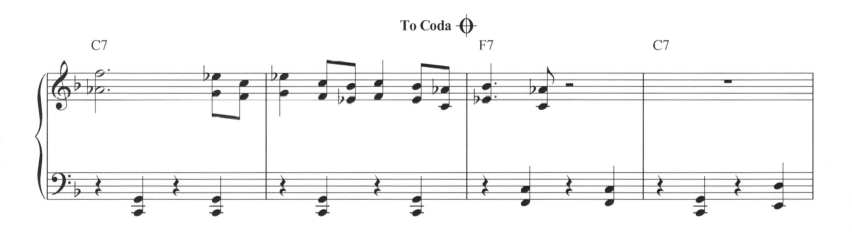

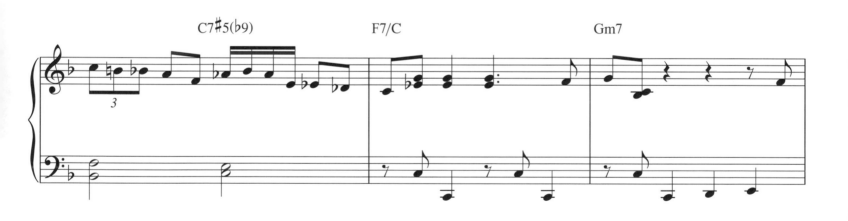

BIRK'S WORKS

By DIZZY GILLESPIE

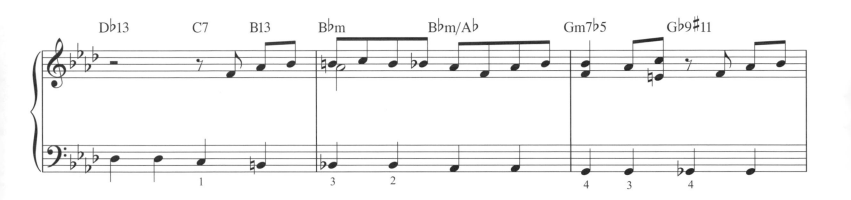

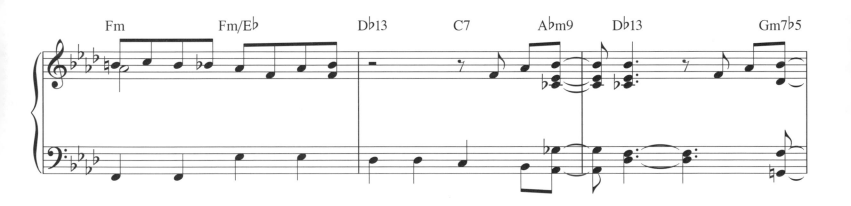

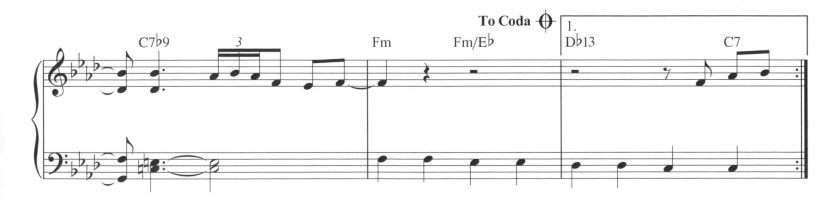

BLUE TRAIN
(Blue Trane)

By JOHN COLTRANE

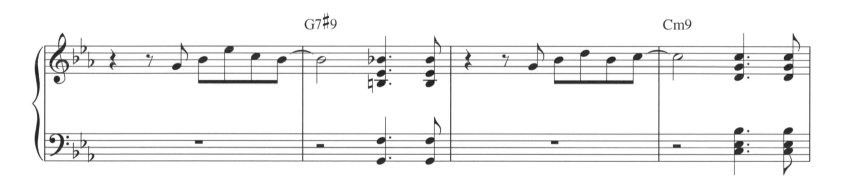

BLUE 'N BOOGIE

By JOHN "DIZZY" GILLESPIE
and FRANK PAPARELLI

BLUE MONK

By THELONIOUS MONK

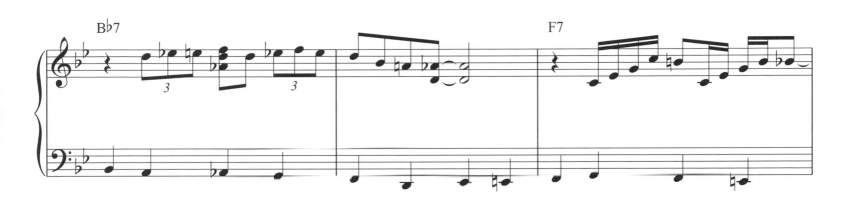

BLUE SEVEN

By SONNY ROLLINS

BLUES BY FIVE

By RED GARLAND

BLUES FOR ALICE

By CHARLIE PARKER

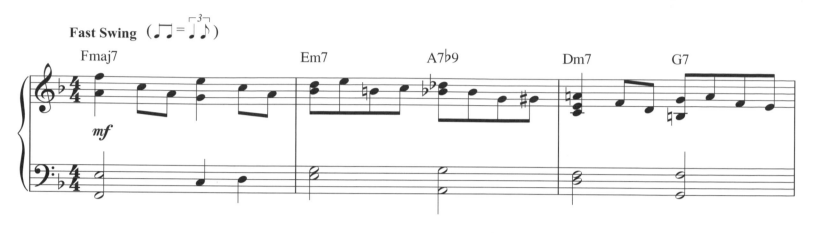

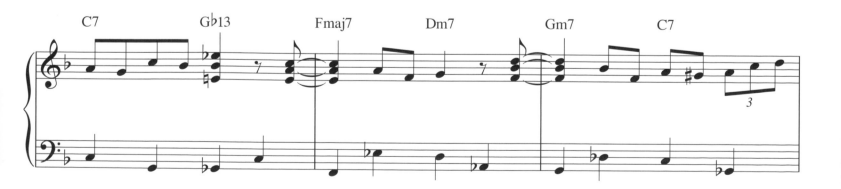

D.C. al Coda

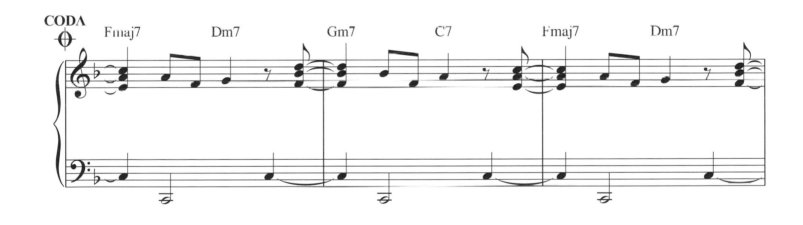

BLUES IN THE CLOSET

By OSCAR PETTIFORD

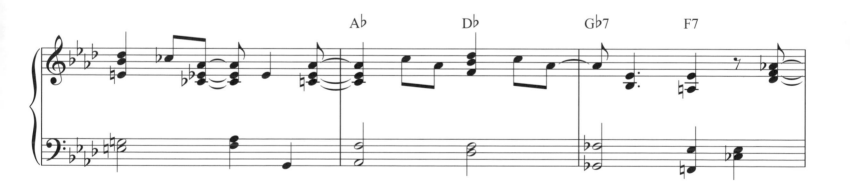

46

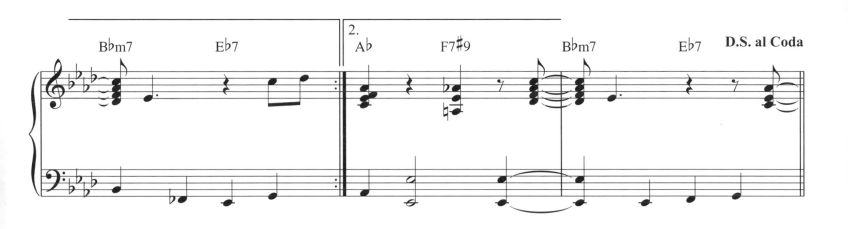

C-JAM BLUES

By DUKE ELLINGTON

Medium Swing

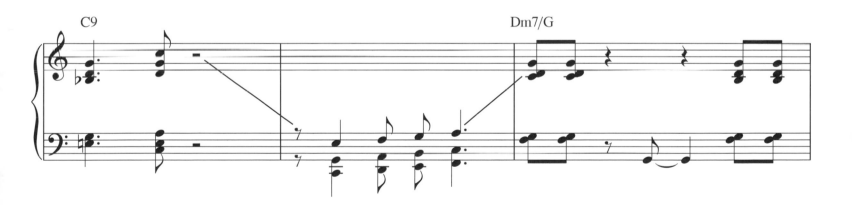

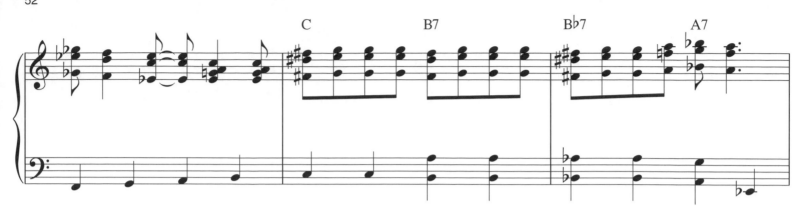

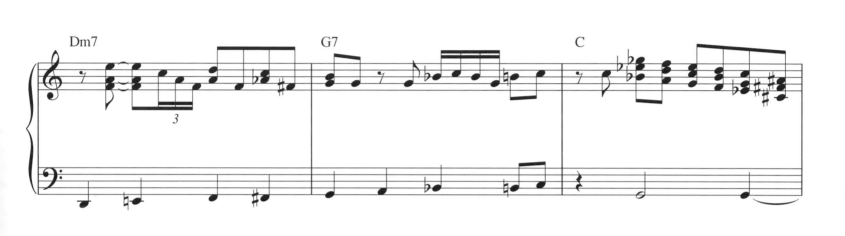

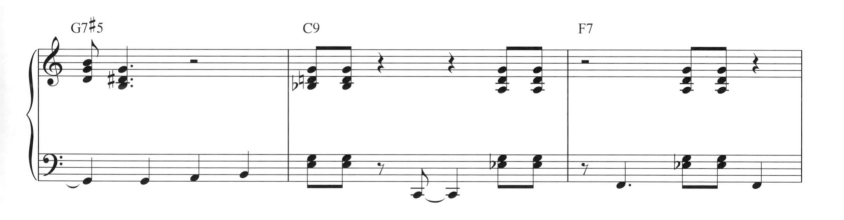

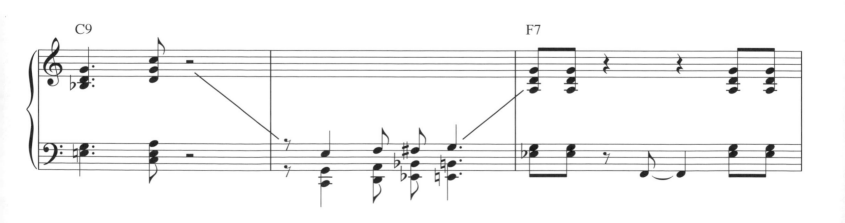

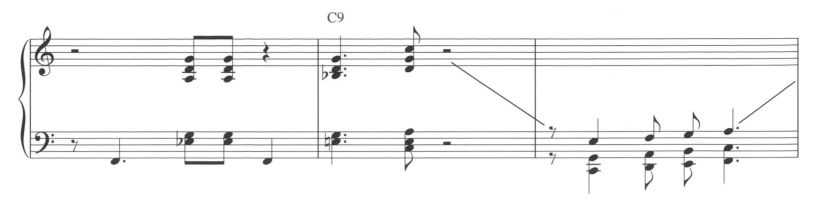

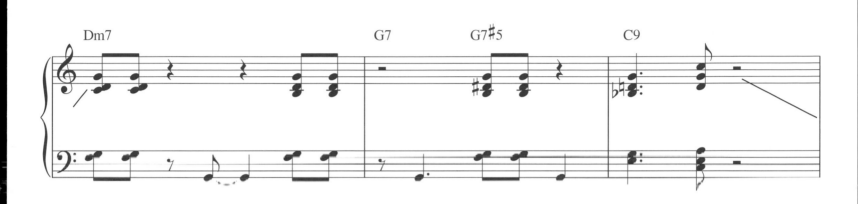

COMIN' HOME BABY

Words and Music by ROBERT DOROUGH
and BENJAMIN TUCKER

D NATURAL BLUES

By JOHN L. (WES) MONTGOMERY

FREDDIE FREELOADER

By MILES DAVIS

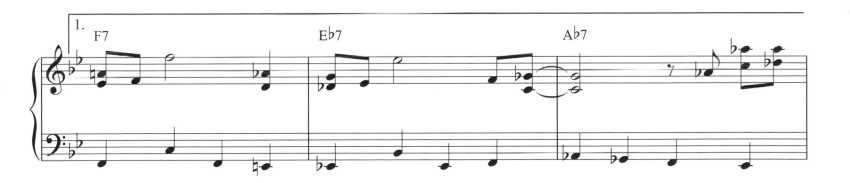

K.C. BLUES

By CHARLIE PARKER

66

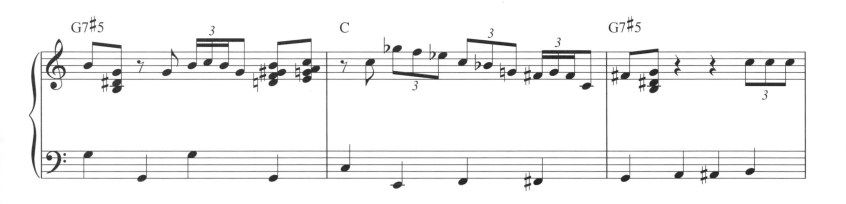

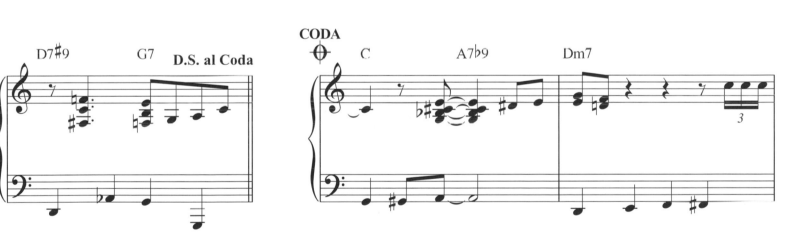

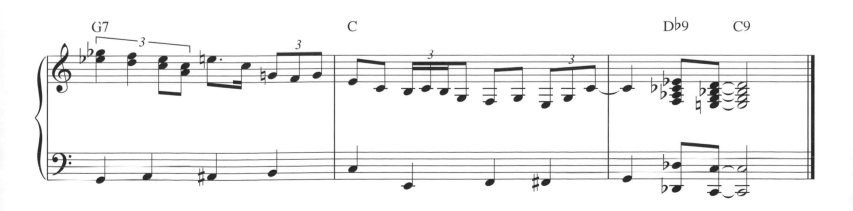

MR. P.C.

By JOHN COLTRANE

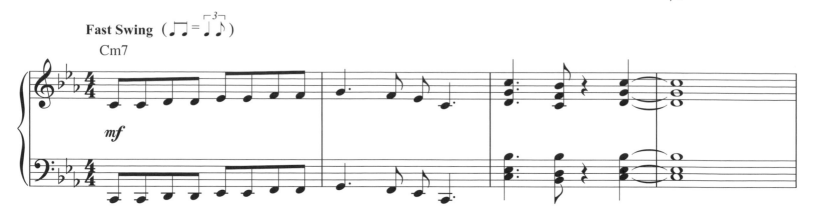

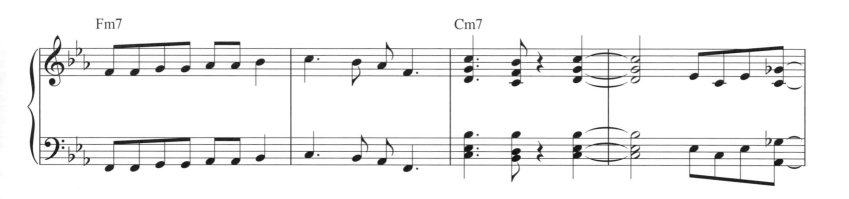

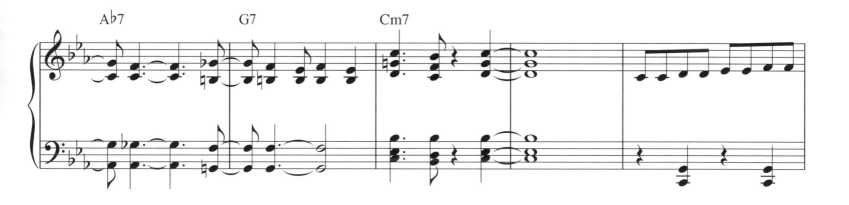

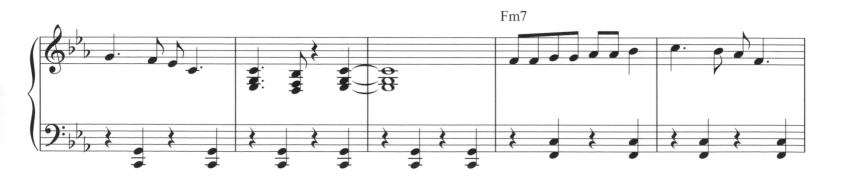

NOW SEE HOW YOU ARE

By OSCAR PETTIFORD
and WOODY HARRIS

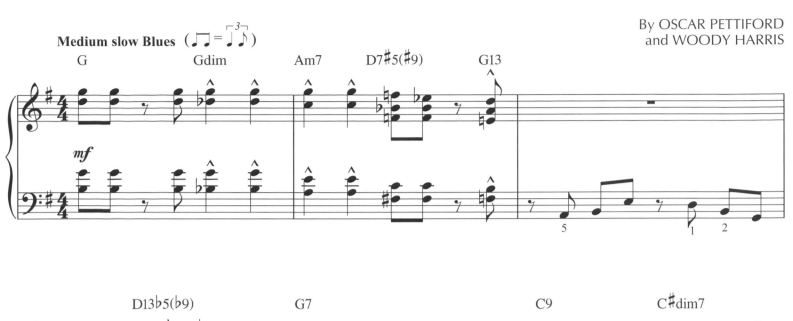

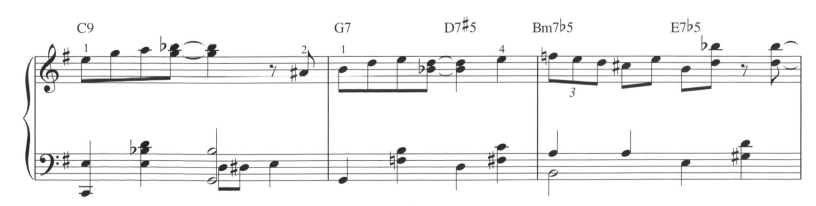

72

NOW'S THE TIME

By CHARLIE PARKER

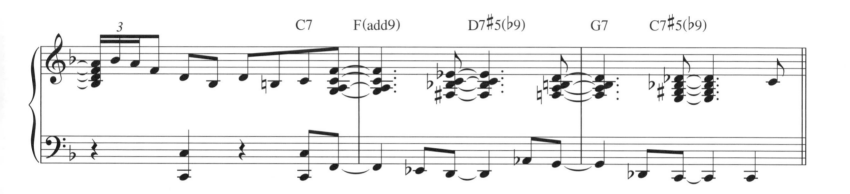

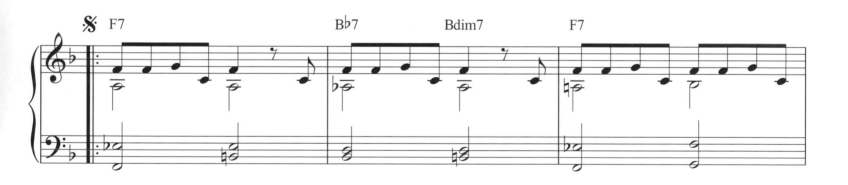

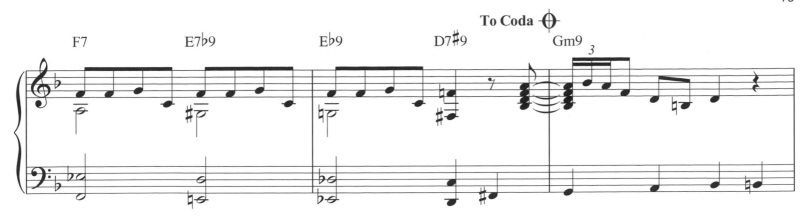

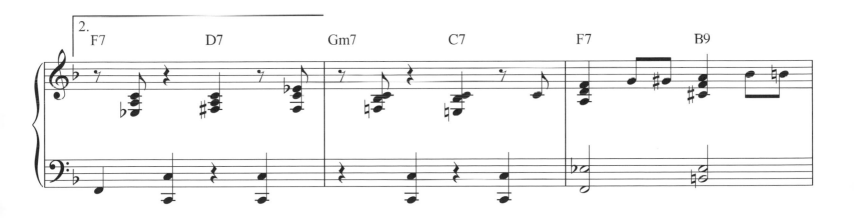

76

STRAIGHT NO CHASER

By THELONIOUS MONK

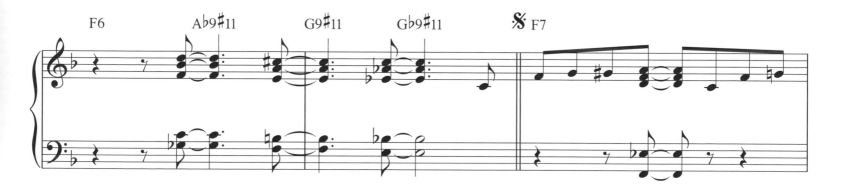

79

TENOR MADNESS

By SONNY ROLLINS

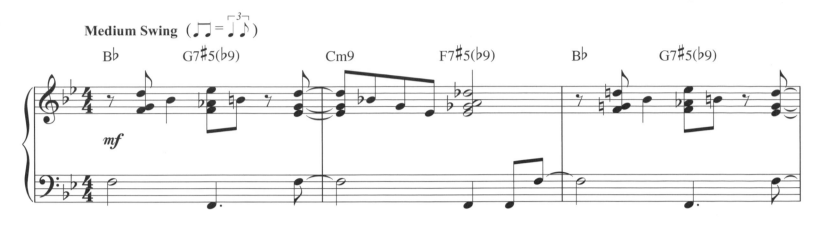

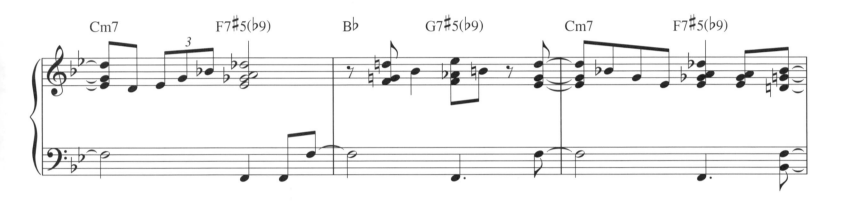

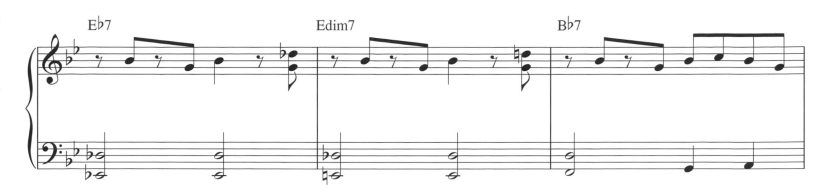

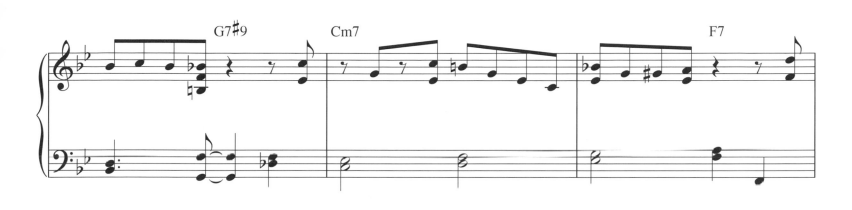

THINGS AIN'T WHAT THEY USED TO BE

By MERCER ELLINGTON

TWO DEGREES EAST,
THREE DEGREES WEST

By JOHN LEWIS

TURNAROUND

By ORNETTE COLEMAN

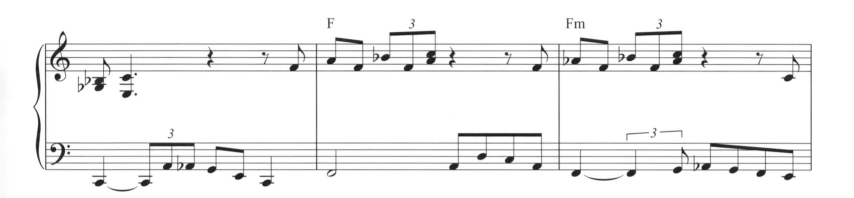

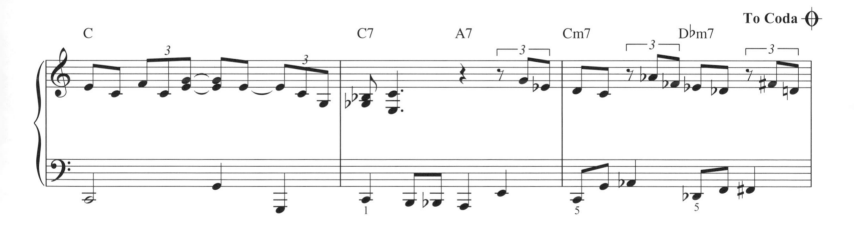

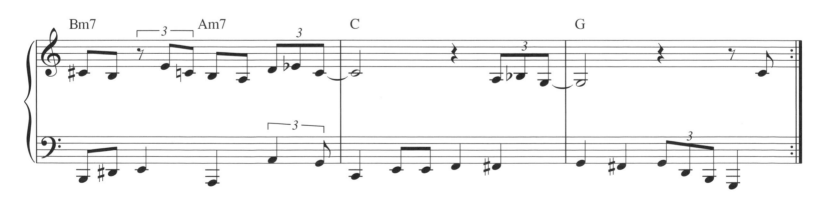

96